HOW TO
MAKE YOUR PAYCHECK LAST

THE COMPLETE, STEP BY STEP GUIDE
TO PERSONAL AND FAMILY FINANCIAL
SUCCESS.

INCLUDING

- 6 Secrets of Successful Financial Planning
- Complete Financial Plan
- Setting Goals That Work
- The 5 Financial Danger Signs

PLUS

- 17 Proven Ways to Change Financial Problems
  into Financial Success
- 7 Rules for Easy Credit Control
- How "To It" Can Work for You
- Dozens of Dollar Stretching Ideas

● Checklists ● Guides ● And much more ●

HOW TO

Make Your Paycheck Last

by
HAROLD MOE

HARSAND FINANCIAL PRESS • WISCONSIN

HOW TO MAKE YOUR PAYCHECK LAST

Published April, 1983
Second Printing 1985

HARSAND FINANCIAL PRESS
N8565 Holseth Road
P.O. Box 515
Holmen, Wisconsin 54636

PRINTED IN THE UNITED STATES OF AMERICA

There is no dignity quite so impressive, and no independence quite so important, as living within your means.

CALVIN COOLIDGE

I would like to thank the bankers, lawyers, CPA's, consultants, brokers, insurance agents & accountants for motivating me to develop a simpler method.

Years ago, as a new co-pilot, I asked seasoned captains for their financial advice. What I heard didn't make sense — why were so many of these well paid pilots broke before their next payday? They earned a lot of money, but didn't have any plan or goals . . . they wanted "it" all, and all at the same time.

So, I started talking to the professional money people . . . accountants, attorneys, CPA's, bankers, and investment counselors. But, all I found were complicated, unrealistic theories . . . without any simple methods. So Sandy (my wife) and I started to develop our own workable system. Where did we start? That was easy - we wrote down what we wanted. These became "goals" — a home in the country, a vacation, and getting out of debt ... goals just like yours.

Next we decided WHAT we wanted FIRST. We didn't always agree on "which" came first, but we found that talking over coffee at our kitchen table was all it required. Actually, going out to our favorite restaurant worked best because we were both on neutral ground. Besides, everyone has a better outlook when they don't have to fix the meal or wash the dishes.

Once we developed this simple and easy system, it was merely a short time before we took a ski vacation in Europe, built our home in the country, and made investments. . . and we were getting out of debt, to boot. Best of all, financially it made us an unbeatable couple, and it can do the same for you.

Over a thousand people are on my plan now. Most are using the companion workbook — which really gets you going and keeps you organized. Just so you have the best possible start, we have included a coupon which makes the Workbook free when you send postage and handling. When your workbook arrives . . . you're on the way to success.

You'll be able to see your total financial situation as far as a full year into the future.

You CAN do it! Stick with it!

HRM

People using the plan say -

Thanks to you and your plan, I can see the light at the end of the tunnel!

Single parent, Minnesota

I love being in control! Believe me, if you earn a paycheck you should have this book! Send another copy as a gift to a wayward friend.

Airline employee, Illinois

I was doing fine until I took a 20% paycut. Your book saved the day.

Worker, Florida

You must tell people! Your book does wonders. I have just returned from a vacation to Israel after using your strategy for only 18 months.

Nurse, Ohio

Have just finished one month with your book, and what an easy way to set up our finances!

Airline Captain, Minnesota

After using MAKE YOUR PAYCHECK LAST, I have control of my financial future. I am making things happen instead of letting things happen . . .

Flight Attendant, Michigan

The new "luxuries" (weekend trips) are something we never would have been able to afford before we started using your plan. The children's educations and a new car are only part of the things we are saving for, instead of worrying about it. Thank you for your book.

Parents, Ohio

. . . We've already done various things you've suggested in your book, but now I think it will all be drawn together into one solid plan.

Homemaker, Hawaii

Retirement has not been (financially) easy, but after reading your book and putting your method to work we are able to live without worry.

Retired, New Mexico

I am currently trying to start over again. Thanks to your book, it's working.

Bankrupt — Chapter 13, Wisconsin

Reading your book together has made us a team.

Housewife, Tennessee

I've read a lot of financial books. This one really works. My only regret is that I didn't buy this book first.

Corporate Executive, Wisconsin

I read about (your) kit in The Wall Street Journal . . . The book fits my criteria for books that work.

WSJ reader, Oklahoma

Your plan works . . . and works as easily as you said it would.

State Patrolman, Wisconsin

This is the very first time I have ever written anyone to tell them how excited I am about their product. Your book is the best thing that has happened to my paycheck in a long time.

Working Single, Minnesota

. . . I never dreamed anything would work for me. But, so far, so good . . .

Secretary, Texas

Praise from the professionals -

We give this a four star value rating. Don't pass it up.

Editor, Washington

I have made strong recommendations to several clients to adopt your program.

Financial Consultant, Colorado

In all my research, I have never seen a more discriptive, easy to follow plan. I wish I would have had your book ten years ago.

Financial Planning Institution President, Wisconsin

. . . members who ordered the kit began saving through payroll deduction, and we received many new accounts because of this kit. We felt that this served as a beneficial financial tool to our members.

Credit Union President, California

Our Credit Union made available to our members the "Financial Strategy Kit" which includes the book, How To Make Your Paycheck Last. *The reaction and results were great! Members who ordered the kit started saving more via payroll deduction and most opened new accounts.*

Credit Union Marketing Director,
Arizona

The book is concise and clear, and the support materials are what has been missing in other approaches to helping the lay person do a better job with personal finances.

Educator, Colorado

My wife and I sat up last night until 2 AM discussing our goals...what an education!

Ph.D., Wisconsin

Make Your Paycheck Last gets people to think about things they want out of their life . . . not just taking things as they come.

Accountant, Wisconsin

Dedicated to everyone who WORKS for their paycheck.

TABLE OF CONTENTS

Where to start . . .
an introduction

Everyone feels a sense of pride and satisfaction when a positive step is taken toward confronting a problem. Your personal money management is no exception. It's taking that first step, making the commitment, that starts the good feelings.

Congratulations! You *should* feel good. 90% of our population knows very little about money management, to say nothing about doing something about it. 80% of the population has never had a savings account. Only 10% of our total population controls how they spend their money. That's what I am going to show you.

As a financial consultant I have met many

people who, like yourself, have recognized the importance of getting control of their money. Recognizing this importance is the FIRST step to getting the most out of your income and then learning how to control it to get what *you want* from your work efforts.

During the past ten years I have constructed personal financial plans for people of every background. People just like you . . . all with the same objective . . . to get a better grip on their money. In this book I will introduce you to the same type of financial plan, at a much lower cost. The price is understandably lower because I am not able to sit down with you and use the spoken word. Instead we communicate on paper. It's still the same plan, only quieter and that could be a better deal for you.

What will we be talking about? Well, we begin where you are. Most people have some information to start with, while others are just now realizing they should (or must) do something to get better control of their money.

You may have noticed that I call my method a plan and not a budget. That's for a very good reason, and it goes like this.

A budget is a monthly system that says you have so much money to spend on food, so much money for entertainment, so much for rent, and so on. Many people put that amount of cash in an envelope marked *Food*, another marked *Entertainment*, a third marked *Rent*, etc. That's a budget and it works. However, it tends to be time limited. That is, it tends to last only a given length of time: while you're in college, during a financial crisis, military service, or the first (or last) years of marriage. The numerous steps required to maintain this type of budget is the principal reason it tends to be so limited.

At one time or another, most people I have worked with used the "self-sealing envelope" budget.

Other people have used a book to record each dollar that gets spent. I used this system when I was in school. In recording everything I was spending, I really was not budgeting. I was recording dollar amounts *AFTER* we parted company. Likewise, using either method I have described, does not tell me how much money I will need in six months, or whether I can make it that far at my present rate of spending. These methods only tell me, *"You have this much money to spend and when it's gone . . . that's it until next pay day!"*

Any method you may have been using to account for your monthly spending is valuable. You will be putting that information to valuable use in the next two chapters.

On the other hand, if you don't have any records or past budgeting experience, that's OK! You may very well do better since you haven't experienced *Pay Day Trauma*, which results in poor self-control and questionable spending practices.

What considerations should be given to a good financial plan? If you're like most people, you'll want your plan to not only record what you're spending, but also provide information so you can:

1) Accurately determine how much income you will need to meet obligations six or even twelve months from now. At the same time, you will want to measure your progress each month (and pat yourself on the back as your monthly progress proves to be right on target).

2) *Actively* plan for those things you someday would like. That's right! Actively do something today to bring you closer to where you want to be tomorrow.

3) Have *all* your monthly obligations in front of you on one display. There are some real benefits to doing this. Most people find they are in better financial shape than they had feared. If your fears are confirmed, you now have the means to recognize its cause.

4) Have a system that quickly shows where you have the spending control you want. Likewise, a system that will show when and *where* spending is getting out of hand.

5) Have a plan that will reward you each month in *extra*, real money as you continue to use it. To say nothing about that terrific feeling of being a winner!

6) Have a plan that doesn't require all your free time to manage. Once you begin using this plan you will need no more than one hour each month. That's all . . . 60 minutes a month! That's not much. If you use more time it's probably because you are watching TV or better yet, patting yourself on the back for a job well done. 60 minutes . . . that averages only 15 minutes each week and just look what you have in return. Think about it. Isn't having control of your spending worth an hour a month? Of course it is!

No, I don't call this a budget, but rather a plan you construct to meet your particular needs. So, find three sheets of paper, a pencil, and clear the kitchen table so we can get started. If you're short on paper use the idea sheet at the end of each chapter.

One last thought before we begin. This system works 100% of the time for 100% of the people that are on my program. The reason being, I proceed one step at a time, never charging ahead until each step is complete. Since I am not able to be with you, it is *very* important for you to proceed one step at a time. There is no time limit! I tested this book method and got the same great results...*AS LONG AS EVERYONE PROCEEDS STEP BY STEP*. If you will do that, I promise you will have the control you want over your money. As a bonus, you'll have that great feeling of confidence and satisfaction that comes from taking charge of your paycheck.

OK, step one is: Find that pencil, the kitchen table, and pour a cup of coffee. I take mine black, thank you, and let's begin with Chapter One.

REMEMBER . . .

YOUR SOMEDAY BEGINS TODAY

Chapter One
It's not what you make that counts!

Ten years ago my wife, Sandra, and I sat down at our kitchen table and asked ourselves, "Where are we *really* going, what do we *really* want, and how do we intend to get there?" Each week we had just enough money until the next paycheck. Sometimes not. We didn't have money in the bank . . . we knew we should . . . we tried a couple of times . . . after all, how could we buy a house without it?

Our car needed attention. It was a Chevy Impala with a crumpled fender that used a quart of transmission fluid a week.

We were making payments to Sears on our stove and refrigerator. There were twenty other things we needed (or wanted) and our daughter was soon to be a reality.

There always was something important to buy. That's when I came across, "It's not what you make that counts, it's what you do with what you make that counts".

Over the years I have modified that springboard quote until it includes, "Plan ahead to get ahead".

Sandra and I took that advice and in 12 months

we moved into our first home. Best of all, our mortgage was our *ONLY* debt.

Our complete story is told in the book, *HOW WE LIVED ON A BUDGET 10 YEARS AND STAYED MARRIED.*

How did we achieve such a task in so short a time? In a word, we made buying a home our number one priority, as opposed to all those THINGS that kept us from getting it a year or two earlier. *We* made our home *our goal.*

Answer these questions to better understand how it works:

1. *Why do you think a budget can help you? Why are you reading this book? What is the outcome you expect?*

2. *Why do you go to work every day? What's it going to get you in ten years? Where do you want to be in ten years?*

3. *What are the things you talk only to yourself about . . . or your best friend . . . or your spouse?*

Let your mind go jogging a few minutes and listen to what it comes up with. These ideas are full of promise and hope. It doesn't matter if it's a little thing like a new coat, or a big deal like a vacation retreat. What is important is that it's important to you!

Remember the times you've said, "Sometime,

wouldn't it be great to . . .", or "Someday I'm going to . . ."? You fill in the spaces.

I've found this question is a real idea starter, "What would you choose to do with your time, if it were yours?"

Now, understand that if what you have *described* can be acknowledged as a realistic goal, it's 99% certain that you can achieve it. Just how is this done? First, write it down. Make a written description of what you want or where you want your life to go.

What does all this have to do with a Financial Plan? Plenty, since you want to take control of your financial future. After all, there is nothing wrong with getting bills paid. But the bigger question is, "How did you get there in the first place and why?" Why not get your finances in order and then keep things going in your *chosen* direction?

The illustration on the next page will be helpful in understanding how goal setting works. Take a moment to study it.

There is just one thing to understand. Goals come in three sizes. There are the long term goals, medium term goals, and short term goals.

Incidentally, words that you might substitute for goals are hopes, plans, expectations, or purpose.

It's too late to begin planning retirement income

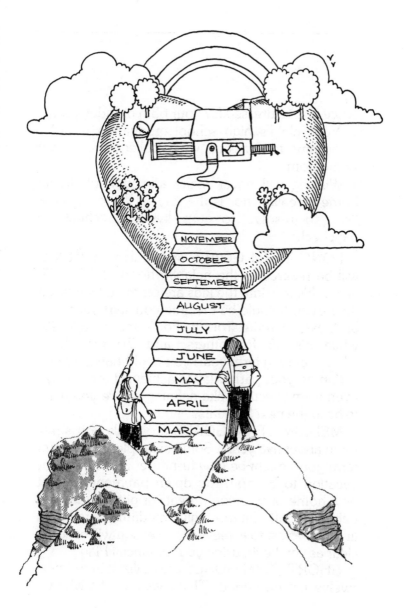

once you're dressed for your 65th birthday party.

Your child's high school graduation is not a good time to consider where college money will come from.

Wishing will never make any type of dream home a reality, nor is the day of the pink slip a time to resolve to stop living paycheck to paycheck.

LONG TERM GOALS are goals you set that will be realized in the neighborhood of 15 to 20 years. It's the time the kids are off to college or on their own. It could be the time you start your own business, or retire from it. For some it's age 40, while it's 55 for others, and 70 for some. Whatever long term goals you might have, it takes *action* on your part today to achieve it tomorrow - even a small action, like defining where you want to be in the next 20 years.

MEDIUM TERM GOALS are goals you strive for in about five years. Some examples of medium term goals might be new furniture, a camper van, vacation to Europe, the down payment on that new home or vacation retreat, or getting that bad debt paid off. Interestingly, medium term goals are the easiest to achieve. The reason will become clear as you begin using your Financial Plan.

SHORT TERM GOALS are realized in the next twelve month period. There was a time when a short term goal was thought to be five or ten years down the road. Actually, that was true only a generation ago. Today the pace of society has accelerated to the point that to want anything is to want it now. Even if it jeopardizes plans for the next several years. Unrealistic short term expectations cause most financial crises that arise in the course of our everyday lives. The first danger signs are statements like,

"I really do *need* that today."
(or)
"I suppose it really wouldn't pay
to fix up the old one."
(or)
"It's so pretty!"
(or)
"This is a once-in-a-lifetime chance."
(or)
"The payments aren't all that big."
(or)
"You go around only once."
(or)
"It's just this once."
(or)
"I owe it to myself."
(or)
"I know I can't afford it, but. . ."

(or)
"Why not?"
(or)
"I simply must have that now."

Whenever you start thinking this sort of self-defeating nonsense, take two aspirin and go straight to bed. Stay there until the urge passes.

A short term goal could be a new living room chair, paying off a charge account, or siding the house.

How do you determine if your goal's realistic? No problem. Your goals will prove themselves when they are tested with your Financial Plan in the next two chapters.

Your goals are important. They give you purpose and direction. Goals enable you to identify what you want and the direction you would like your life to go. They are the most important part of any sound Financial Plan, and in a family situation, goals bring unity in effort, since everyone knows the objective and can pull together.

If you do nothing today to bring yourself closer to where you want to be tomorrow, tomorrow will come in spite of your reluctance. Each of us is different. That's good! However, we each have 24 hours in our day. The President has 24 hours a day, I have 24 hours a day, and you have the same 24 hours. No more, no less. It's what you do with what you have that's important. What you *don't* have is not important. Without a goal, no budget or financial plan can possibly work. Without a goal, there is nothing to come true. Your *purpose* is important.

STEP TWO: Take one of your three sheets of paper, or the idea sheet at the end of this chapter, and write LONG TERM GOALS at the top. If you're married, your spouse should make a separate list. Do your own writing and don't compare lists until you have completed this entire step. List your long term goals from 1 through a limit of 10. Usually, you are lucky to come up with 3 long term goals. However, do not exceed a list of 10. By limiting yourself to 10 you won't become overwhelmed. It's much like working around the house on Saturday morning. If you have 3 or 4 projects to get done, they are completed in short order. On the other hand, if there are 20 jobs to complete, you become so overwhelmed by it all that you simply fold up your tent and collapse on the couch before you ever get started.

On sheet number two, make a list of your medium term goals. What would you like to accomplish within the next five years? Take your time and let your mind wander. Again, limit yourself to a list of not more than ten goals. 7 or 8 goals are about average.

Finally, on sheet number three list those objectives you want to achieve over the next twelve months. Again, limit yourself to the ten most important goals. Usually 15 or 20 ideas will come to mind. The extra can be incorporated next year. Only the ten hottest ones for now!

Look over your lists one more time. Once you are satisfied with your selections, compare yours with your spouse. RULE ONE: Don't criticize your spouse's list. You are sincere with yours and so is your spouse. Accept it as being what your spouse really feels.

It is now time to combine the two LONG TERM GOALS lists into one. The principal wage earner starts with goal one and each in turn adds one goal to the combined list until it becomes a list of *ten* (or less). Do the same with the MEDIUM and SHORT TERM lists.

If, during the next few days, you think it over and want to change a goal, do so. But, only ones that you contributed to the list, unless you both are in agreement.

Remember your goals! That is so important. I know people who memorize theirs. Others display them where the bills are paid, or on the bathroom mirror. Whatever works for you is fine. Remember your goals — it's an important ingredient for the success of your Financial Plan.

An example is worth a thousand words. In this case, the story of Bill and Mary Stevenson can illustrate what I have just talked about. Bill and Mary's story is real. I have changed their names only because it seemed like the right thing to do.

Bill is a teacher and brings home $1040.00 per month. Mary works part-time at her father's flower shop. Their story is the example we will follow throughout this book in setting up your own Financial Plan. Their dollar amounts may appear to be a little low because I am using their initial plan which now is several years old. However, the plan is valid for this example because the percentages remain the same.

After I met the Stevenson's, it was clear their situation was not as hopeless as Bill had described. He called it desperate, but I calmly reminded him that I am the expert and we will call it average - LIKE YOURS. It is never as bad as it first seems. On the other hand, I realize it's no bed of roses, either.

So much for the introduction. On the following page (*Illustration 2*) you will see a reprint of what the Stevenson's arrived at after combining their goal lists.

Bill and Mary's lists are well done. Take the time

SHORT TERM GOALS — 12 months

1.	Pay off Visa	$ 750.00
2.	End surprise bills - Insurance, Medical, etc.	
3.	Car Cassette Player	210.00
4.	Develop a closer relationship as a couple	
5.	Get spending under control	
6.	Hide-A-Bed for living room	300.00
7.	Refinishing sander	60.00
8.	X-Country Skis (Mary)	125.00
9.	Winterize car	200.00
10.	Refinish dining room table	
		$1645.00

MEDIUM TERM GOALS - 5 years

1.	Honda motorcycle	$ 950.00
2.	Financial security from strikes and medical emergencies	2000.00
3.	Down payment on home	4000.00
4.	Have baby	1000.00
5.	New car down payment	600.00
6.	Replace bedroom set	800.00
7.	Color TV	400.00
		$9750.00

LONG TERM GOALS - 15 years

1.	Be established in university level education	
2.	Vacation to England	$5000.00
	ILLUSTRATION 2	**$5000.00**

to thoroughly review their lists. They talked about each goal and both felt satisfied with them. In a year, or less, they will sit down to review their lists and evaluate their progress. At that time they may make changes to all lists. That's good! It shows they are thinking and growing. Priorities and goals change just as we change as individuals.

Besides dating their lists, whenever a dollar value could be assigned, they made a ball park guess.

IN SUMMARY:

1) When making goal lists, start with the LONG TERM GOALS first.
2) Your goal lists should be kept in a handy place for frequent reference and encouragement.
3) If you are married, work together and agree that your goals are *worthy* of everyone involved.
4) Each year our lives change and so will some goals. Remain as flexible as possible.
5) Year after year, continue to save your goal list. They are your best measure of progress.
6) Remember your goals. It's not just a matter of priority, but the success of your Financial Plan *depends* on it.

Congratulations again! You have completed the most difficult part of constructing your Financial

Plan. Armed with your three goal lists, let's continue to Chapter Two.

REMEMBER . . .

ADD A LITTLE GOAL TO YOUR LIFE

IDEAS AND NOTES
It's not what you make that counts.

1. Will I need the Financial Workbook?

Chapter Two
It's what you do with what you make that counts!

Located in your Financial Plan Workbook are several legal sized sheets titled *Financial Plan*. They are divided into four sections: *Savings, Obligations, Net Income* and *Surplus*. This is the form you will use to construct your Financial Plan. The original copy of your Financial Plan usually requires some adjustment, so another sheet can be used for a more legible final draft. When you run out, use the order form in the back of this book.

Let's begin with the section titled *Obligations*. These are the *Monthly* payments to the butcher, the baker and anyone else. This is where any records you might have are invaluable...check registers, budget records, expense records, a keen memory, etc.

To illustrate how this section is completed, follow along with the Stevenson's example on the next page, Illustration 3. Bill and Mary have listed all the areas they spend money each month.

FINANCIAL PLAN

REAL & PROJECTED

SAVINGS

YEAR	JAN	FEB	MAR	APR	MAY	JUN	JUL	AUG	SEPT	OCT	NOV	DEC
1ST FEDERAL SAVINGS & LOAN		248-	248-	248-	248-	248-						
STATE BANK		75-	75-	75-	75-	75-						

OBLIGATIONS

	JAN	FEB	MAR	APR	MAY	JUN	JUL	AUG	SEPT	OCT	NOV	DEC
RENT		170-	170-	170-	170-	170-						
ELECTRIC COMPANY		31-	31-	31-	31-	31-						
TELEPHONE		33-	33-	33-	33-	33-						
GIFTS AND CONTRIBUTIONS		16-	16-	16-	16-	16-						
HOUSEHOLD		165-	165-	165-	165-	165-						
CAR PAYMENT		60-	60-	60-	60-	60-				52-		
STEREO PAYMENT		21-	21-	21-	21-	21-			17-			
CHARGE PAYMENT VISA SEARS CITGO		180-	180-	180-	180-	180-						
SCHOOL EXPENSE - BILL		40-	40-	40-	40-	40-						
RECREATION AND ENTERTAINMENT		35-	35-	35-	35-	35-						
MISC		65-	65-	65-	65-	65-						
TOTAL OBLIGATIONS		1139-	1139-	1139-	1139-	1139-						

NET INCOME

	JAN	FEB	MAR	APR	MAY	JUN	JUL	AUG	SEPT	OCT	NOV	DEC
BILL		1040-	1040-	1040-	1040-	1040-			1060-			
MARY		115-	115-	115-	115-	115-				140-	140-	140-
TOTAL INCOME		1155-	1155-	1155-	1155-	1155-						

SURPLUS

	JAN	FEB	MAR	APR	MAY	JUN	JUL	AUG	SEPT	OCT	NOV	DEC
		16-	16-	16-	16-	16-						

ILLUSTRATION NUMBER 3

RENT is self explanatory since they live in a one bedroom, unfurnished apartment. The $170.00 is written in small numbers at the top of the square to the right of the rent title. This amount is really a projection of what Bill and Mary *plan* to spend. After they write their rent check, the *actual* amount is entered in large numbers.

If you are a home owner, *MORTGAGE* would be the appropriate title for your entry.

Notice also, the Stevenson's didn't start their Plan until February, so January entries were left blank.

ELECTRIC COMPANY: The Stevenson's are on the budget plan and project a cost of $31.00 each month for light and electric heat. Budget plans are a great help in financial planning. If you are unable to subscribe to such a plan (they go by several names), use past receipts to estimate seasonal fluctuations. Add 10% to your last year's cost for an inflation factor, or your utility company can give you an accurate idea of what to expect this year.

Many heating oil companies also offer budget helper plans. It's worth asking about.

TELEPHONE bills are directly controlled by you. When there is a need to reduce spending, your phone is a good place to start. Sending a post card or letter is an easy way to put you back on firm financial ground without upsetting your standard of living.

Most telephone companies offer a call-pack type promotion. Where considerable long distance calling is necessary, this service can reduce charges up to about 50%.

GIFTS AND CONTRIBUTIONS are charitable or religious donations made on a more or less regular basis.

HOUSEHOLD: Mary plans and buys the groceries and household supplies. The projected $165.00 also includes an amount for Mary to spend as she sees fit. More about this category later.

CAR PAYMENT is a coupon type installment payment. Each coupon book payment should be listed separately. Also, as you can see in illustration 3, their car will be paid off in October of this year.

STEREO: The stereo package is another coupon payment that will end in September.

CHARGE PAYMENTS: One short term goal Bill and Mary have is to pay off Visa this year. If you haven't taken the time, read over their goal lists in Chapter One. I will be making several references to it in this section.

They also have Sears and Citgo credit cards. Both have mutually agreed to discontinue using their Visa and Sears cards until they are paid off. Since Bill and Mary get gas at their neighborhood Citgo station, they feel a credit card is more convenient than cash. The $180.00 projected payment is computed this way: Bill placed paying Visa ($750.00) as his first *short* term goal. $750.00 divided by twelve months means that $64.00 per month will meet that goal. Sears gets $40.00. Both Visa and Sears payments are greater than the required minimum. They pay their Citgo bill, which averages $76.00, in full each month and that all totalled comes to $180.00.

Looks good and they have met their first short term goal as a bonus!

SCHOOL EXPENSES: Bill uses this money to buy some meals at school, as well as other school related expenses. He feels the $40.00 projection will leave something for him to spend as he sees fit.

ENTERTAINMENT can be a tough cookie! Originally Bill and Mary actually spent $195.00 per month on their entertainment. From the first draft of their Financial Plan, it was clear there just wasn't enough cash to go around. After reviewing their goals and monthly obligations, they felt entertainment was their best candidate for adjustment.

Instead of eating out each week they plan for twice a month. If there is any money left in *SUR-PLUS* they *may* eat out more. Entertainment was very important to Bill and Mary. Eating out, movies, and plays were a large part of their lifestyle. After they considered their goals, they found that entertainment was one of the biggest contributing factors to their somewhat delicate financial condition.

Bill and Mary also found a new word — *RECREATION.* It costs less than entertainment. Bike riding, tennis, walks in the park, and the municipal pool now supplement entertainment to help keep their costs in line. Additionally, the Stevenson's found that recreation, as a couple, helps realize their fourth *short term* goal.

*MISC*ellaneous is a catchall for those unanticipated expenses. All Financial Plans should include this heading. Bill and Mary include subscriptions and occasional drug store prescriptions in this category.

If any single item *consistently* finds it's way into *MISC,* consider adding a separate entry title for it.

Other MONTHLY obligation titles to use if your situation requires:

Child Care	*Utilities*	*Mortgage*
Tuition	*Auto Expense*	*Gasoline*

Laundry	Medical/Dental	Water
Business Expense	Allowances	Alimony
Cleaning Lady	Car Pool	Clothing

STEP THREE: List your *monthly* obligations on your Financial Plan.

At this time, if you do not have a checking account, open one. You will have an excellent record of money spent. Also, a checking account provides a reliable means of controlling spending as well as valuable income tax documentation.

It is a demonstrated fact that using a checking account is more economical and clearly more accurate than paying by cash.

Deposit ALL income into your checking account and make your payments from it. If you're married, two checking accounts will work even better. Bill and Mary use two accounts. The first, or primary account is used to deposit all income. *Monthly* bills and savings are paid from this account. A check is written to Mary for $165.00 which covers *weekly* HOUSEHOLD expenses. She deposits this check in her own checking account. There are several benefits to this arrangement. First, Mary is able to plan and control her spending better than if she has a large amount of cash around. Secondly, a separate checking account gives Mary a greater sense of pride in that she has her own money to spend. As long as she meets her obligation to *HOUSEHOLD* spending she is *never* called to account for how she spends this money. This is also true for Bill and the area of his personal spending. Thirdly, when Bill and Mary evaluate their Financial Plan, they will have a much more accurate record to justify any needed changes in *HOUSEHOLD* spending.

In a family situation, the purchase of the household supplies, groceries, clothes, and related items tend to fall on one person. These expenses will require a greater number of purchases and will be easier to manage with the second checking account.

However, in a situation where one spouse has proven to be unable to exercise the necessary spending control, it is best to use only one checking account.

By this time, you should have plans to open one or even two checking accounts. The first, an absolute necessity, will be used to pay *monthly* obligations. The second account is used for any specialized *weekly* obligation such as household and grocery purchases.

Now, let's see how two SAVINGS accounts can work for you. Each year everyone has payments that surprise and frustrate their best laid plans. Insurance payments head the "There has got to be a better way to handle this" list. There is! By saving a little each month there will be money to make those payments that appear at the most inconvenient intervals.

Examples of these bills are : Taxes, Insurance, Bank Note Payments, Auto Tune-up, Heating Oil (not on a budget plan), Annual School Tuition, Vacation Money, Health Club, Y Membership, etc.

These are all bills we know will arrive, but we may not know when or that there are so many, so often. I have come to call these the NOT SO MONTHLY OBLIGATIONS. Once you have a handle on them they aren't nearly so difficult to work with. How do you figure out how much to save? Illustratively, it looks like this:

BEFORE SAVINGS: AFTER SAVINGS:

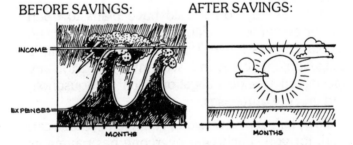

BY SAVING MONTHLY, YOU WILL ELIMINATE THOSE FINANCIAL CRISIS TIMES!

When the Stevenson's prepared their list of *Not So Monthly Obligations,* they included the dollar amount, obligation, and the month the bill arrives. After combining their receipts, recollections, and notes the Stevenson's ended up like this:

THE CRISIS ELIMINATION LIST

$120.00	Contribution to teachers group medical plan	(FEB)
210.00	Auto Insurance	(APR)
148.00	Life Insurance (Bill)	(APR)
131.00	Life Insurance - (Mary)	(JUN)
80.00	Dentist	(AUG)
200.00	Winterize Car (Short Term Goal)	(OCT)

$889.00 Divided by 12 (months) equals $75.00 monthly.

Bill and Mary opened their first savings account at their local bank. Each month Bill writes and deposits a check for $75.00 into this account. Mary had $85.00 already stashed for these expenses and deposited this when they opened their account.

STEP FOUR: List all your *NOT SO MONTHLY*

OBLIGATIONS. To help arrange your short term savings program use the following form to organize your payments. Start with the example bills we discussed at the start of Crisis Elimination. Finally, review your SHORT TERM GOAL list.

Don't list small things like magazine subscriptions, since this is easier to pay out of miscellaneous (OBLIGATIONS section). The Stevensons's chose to put *DENTIST* on their list. You may find it easier to make that payment out of Obligations and not your Short Term Savings. Consider your situation and decide what will work easiest for you.

DIG THEM ALL OUT.

THE CRISIS ELIMINATION LIST

	Amount	Obligation	Month Due:
1.			
2.			
3.			
4.			
5.			
6.			
7.			
8.			
9.			
10.			

$_____ divided by 12 (months)

= $_____

Saved each month in your *Short Term Savings Account* to eliminate the crisis times!

NOTE: Savings and Loans, as well as most banks offer interest on certain *checking accounts.* These accounts are ideal when planning your Crisis Elimination List in that you will receive the same interest as a passbook savings account. But, you can write the necessary checks at home, saving the time and expense of a trip to the bank to make your withdrawal.

Referring to Illustration 3, Bill and Mary entered *State Bank* in the section titled *Savings.* In small numbers they entered $75.00 as the amount projected to be saved in this account each month.

You can see how this savings plan can smooth out the crises that tend to strike every few months.

Your *second* savings account is used to provide opportunity. It will bring you, each month, one step closer to where you want to be tomorrow. To clarify how this is accomplished, follow along as the Stevenson's compute their *Long Term* Savings plan.

On their goal lists, the Stevenson's assigned a dollar cost to all monetary type goals. For convenience, I have included another copy of their goal list on the next page.

As you will recall, Bill and Mary included paying off their Visa account in their *monthly obligations.* The winterization of their car and surprise bills were included in their *Short Term* Savings

SHORT TERM GOALS — 12 months

DONE 1. Pay off Visa $ 750.00
DONE 2. End surprise bills - Insurance,
Medical, etc.
3. Car Cassette Player 210.00
4. Develop a closer relationship as a
couple
5. Get spending under control
6. Hide-A-Bed for living room 300.00
7. Refinishing sander 60.00
8. X-Country Skis (Mary) 125.00
DONE 9. Winterize car 200.00
10. Refinish dining room table
_____
$1645.00

MEDIUM TERM GOALS - 5 years

1. Honda motorcycle $ 950.00
2. Financial security from strikes
and medical emergencies 2000.00
3. Down payment on home 4000.00
4. Have baby 1000.00
5. New car down payment 600.00
6. Replace bedroom set 800.00
7. Color TV 400.00
_____
$9750.00

LONG TERM GOALS - 15 years

1. Be established in university level
education
2. Vacation to England $5000.00
_____
$5000.00

Account. When totaling the *remaining* monetary goals, this is how it shapes up:

$695.00 -The total remaining *Short Term* Goals. Therefore: $695.00 divided by 12 (months) equals $58.00 required per month to realize their remaining *Short Term Goals.*

$9750.00 -The total *Medium Term Goals.* $9750.00 divided by 60 (months i.e. five years) equals $162.00 required per month to realize their *Medium Term Goals.*

$5000.00 -The total of the *Long Term Goals* $5000.00 divided by 180 (months i.e. fifteen years) equals $28.00 per month to realize their *Long Term Goals.*

Next, add the dollar amounts together:

Short Term Goals =	$ 58.00 *per month*
Medium Term Goals =	162.00 *per month*
Long Term Goals =	28.00 *per month*

TOTAL $248.00

On their Financial Plan, Bill and Mary entered a projection of $248.00 in small numbers across from the savings titled *First Federal S&L*. By saving $248.00 per month, the Stevenson's will have the money necessary to meet each of the monetary goals they have set for themselves.

NOTE: These totals do not reflect the interest they will receive on this money while it is in their savings account . . . another bonus!

Another bonus is the fact that their new savings and checking accounts have given the Stevenson's a sound credit base. It will do the same for you.

Do you see the importance of two savings accounts? The first, *a Short Term* Account, is used to smooth out the roughness of the *not so monthly obligations*. The second, a *Long Term* Account, will make your future goals possible. Your checking account provides organization and control, but it's a consistent savings program that will enable you to have the wherewithal to take advantage of opportunity. Do not overlook the absolute importance of a consistent, determined savings program.

STEP FIVE: Complete the savings portions of your Financial Plan. Use the nifty forms on the next pages and enter your projections as the Stevenson's did. These totals will be combined to complete your *Long Term Savings.*

Refer to your three goal lists and include all remaining SHORT TERM goals with a dollar amount.

DOLLAR AMOUNT   SHORT TERM GOAL

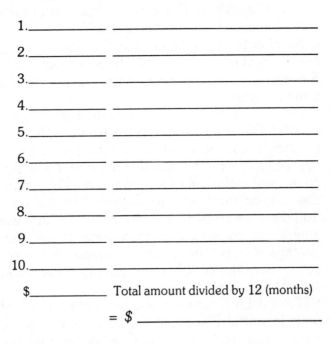

1._____ _____

2._____ _____

3._____ _____

4._____ _____

5._____ _____

6._____ _____

7._____ _____

8._____ _____

9._____ _____

10._____ _____

$_____ Total amount divided by 12 (months)

= $ _____

Refer to your three goal lists and include all remaining MEDIUM TERM goals with a dollar amount.

DOLLAR AMOUNT   MEDIUM TERM GOAL

1._____ _____

2._____ _____

3._____ _____

4._____ _____

5._____ _____

6._____ _____

7._____ _____

8._____ _____

9._____ _____

10._____ _____

$_____Total amount divided by 60 (months)

= $ _____

Refer to your three goal lists and include all remaining LONG TERM goals with a dollar amount.

DOLLAR AMOUNT   LONG TERM GOAL

1._____ _____

2._____ _____

3._____ _____

4._____ _____

5._____ _____

6._____ _____

7._____ _____

8._____ _____

9._____ _____

10._____ _____

$_____Total amount divided by 180 (months)

        = $_____

Next, enter your three goal list totals as follows:

SHORT TERM Goals = $_____ per month

MEDIUM TERM Goals = $_____ per month

LONG TERM Goals = $_____ per month

TOTAL $_____ Deposited
each month into your
LONG TERM Savings
account — your opportunity
account.

Enter your total deposit on your Financial Plan. With that you have completed Step Five!

Before we continue, let's check the coffee one more time.

Bill and Mary now added the projected *SAVINGS* and *OBLIGATIONS* column and entered this single projected total at the bottom of the obligations section titled TOTAL OBLIGATIONS. Referring to Illustration 3, the Stevenson's total projected obligations are $1139.00 per month.

TOTAL YOUR PROJECTIONS.

And now, down to the *NET INCOME SEC-TION*. Net income is the amount of money you bring home (take home pay to some people). Bill brings home $1040, while Mary brings home $115.00, for a total of $1155.00 per month. This is shown under TOTAL INCOME (Illustration 3). In September Bill expects to get a raise which he has indicated in the September income column. Mary works one more day a week in October, November, and December. This increase is also included in their projections.

Indicate any changes you expect throughout the year. This is also true when entering projections for savings and monthly obligations.

STEP SIX: Complete your *INCOME* SECTION BY LISTING YOUR NET INCOME.

Down to the bottom line - *SURPLUS*. What's Surplus? Look at it like this: To this point you have provided for all your monthly obligation, you have saved for those *not so monthly* obligations, and you have saved for the future. Whatever is left is surplus money.

What does a hard working manager of personal finance do with a surplus? Write yourself a check for a job well done.

Over the years, Sandra and I have used our monthly surplus for a canoe, chain saw, a horse, increased savings, and extra dinners out. THE HARDER YOU WORK YOUR FINANCIAL PLAN, THE MORE SURPLUS YOU WILL HAVE!

Subtracting *Total Obligations* from *Total Income* equals *Surplus.*

It is important to take the *surplus* money out of your checking account so that the amount doesn't accumulate. There seems to be a natural tendency to want to let surplus money accumulate for some future moment. Hopefully you will see why this is not a good idea.

Bill and Mary always leave $25.00 in their account to prevent an overdraft. This is a good idea. In reality, this $25.00 *buffer* is a zero balance and is treated as such. When this balance is reached no more money is spent. To see this more clearly, let's assume Bill and Mary let their surplus accumulate to say $45.00. With their $70.00 checking account balance ($45.00 surplus and $25.00 buffer = $70.00) they have occasion to spend $50.00. Suddenly, their Financial Plan is in the red by $5.00, even though their checking account shows a balance of $20.00. NOT GOOD.

By removing *surplus* money from your checking account, you're actually balancing your *checkbook* with your *financial plan.* THAT'S IMPORTANT.

It's a good idea to have a *buffer.* Also, when your Plan has a surplus, remove it. I'll show you how in Chapter Three.

STOP! Be certain you have done the following:
1. Completed each section of your Financial Plan with projections for the first six months.
2. Opened one or two checking accounts.
3. Opened TWO savings accounts.

If your just completed Financial Plan projections show a loss of more than thirty dollars (a negative surplus) go directly to Chapter Four. Do not pass go! Do not refill your coffee cup.

If your Financial Plan projections show a surplus, proceed to Step Seven.

STEP SEVEN: Take a break and I'll see you in Chapter Three.

REMEMBER . . .

IT'S NOT WHAT YOU MAKE THAT COUNTS. IT'S WHAT YOU DO WITH WHAT YOU MAKE THAT COUNTS.

IDEAS AND NOTES
It's what you do with what you make that counts.

Chapter Three
60 minutes of keeping up.

In Chapter Three we'll talk about keeping your Financial Plan up to date, month after month.

Maintaining your Financial Plan is nothing more than entering the amount of money ACTUALLY spent in each category of OBLIGATIONS AND SAVINGS. There are two ways to do this. The first method is simple and the second is easy.

The *first* method is used when *one* check is written per obligation each month. I prefer to use this method to familiarize you with the simplicity of keeping your Plan up to date only. However, if you are single or retired and write no more than one check per month in each category of *OBLIGATION* this method can work for you.

Your checkbook provides a means of recording all the checks you write, either in the form of a copy of your check or a check register. Either way, starting with the first check of the month, enter the actual check amount under your projection for each obligation on your Financial Plan.

After all checks have been entered, total the monthly column. Enter this total under your projection for TOTAL OBLIGATIONS.

Lastly, subtract TOTAL OBLIGATIONS from NET INCOME. The remainder is your SURPLUS.

Simple? YES!

More than likely you will be writing several checks in the categories of MISC, CHARGE PAYMENTS, ENTERTAINMENT, and HOUSEHOLD (should you decide not to use a second checking account).

The *second* method is used to simplify updating your Financial Plan when more than one check is written in *any* category each month. This method offers the advantage of being able to see where most checks are written (control) and, though it takes a little longer, it's actually easier.

Let me illustrate. Bill and Mary ended the month of February by writing 19 checks. The following page is a reproduction of their check register (Illustration 4).

Using a FINANCIAL PLAN WORKSHEET shown in Illustration 5, Bill and Mary titled each column from their Financial Plan.

Then, from their check register, they entered each check by number and description (with the dollar amount entered in the appropriate column).

After all checks are entered, each column is totalled. These totals are the *actual* dollars spent in

RECORD ALL CHARGES OR CREDITS THAT AFFECT YOUR ACCOUNT

NUMBER	DATE	DESCRIPTION OF TRANSACTION	PAYMENT/DEBIT	√ T	FEE IF ANY	DEPOSIT/CREDIT	BALANCE 25 00
	2/1	DEPOSIT (BILL)				520 00	545 00
101	2/1	RENT	170 00				
102	2/1	1ST FEDERAL - SAVINGS	248 00				127 00
	2/6	DEPOSIT (MARY)				115 00	242 00
103	2/5	MARY S.	165 00				
104	2/5	SECOND FINANCE	60 00				17 00

	2/15	DEPOSIT (BILL)				520 00	537 00
105	2/15	STATE BANK	75 00				
106	2/15	BILL S.	40 00				
107	2/15	UNITED FUND	10 00				412 00
108	2/20	READER'S DIGEST	17 40				
109	2/22	SEARS	40 00				
110	2/22	ELECTRIC CO.	26 50				

RECORD ALL CHARGES OR CREDITS THAT AFFECT YOUR ACCOUNT

NUMBER	DATE	DESCRIPTION OF TRANSACTION	PAYMENT/DEBIT	√ T	FEE IF ANY	DEPOSIT/CREDIT	BALANCE 328 10
111	2/22	TELEPHONE CO.	28 00				
112	2/22	VISA	64 00				236 10
113	2/24	CITGO OIL	74 00				
114	2/24	SECOND FINANCE	21 00				
115	2/24	THE NITE CLUB	26 75				114 35
116	2/25	REXALL	38 75				75 60
117	2/28	UNITED CHURCH	6 00				
118	2/28	SPORT SHOP	15 00				54 60
119	2/28	CASH (SURPLUS)	29 60				25 00
		MARCH					
	3/1	DEPOSIT (BILL)				520 00	545 00
120	3/1	RENT	170 00				
121	3/1	CYCLE SHOP	23 50				351 50

REMEMBER TO RECORD AUTOMATIC PAYMENTS / DEPOSITS ON DATE AUTHORIZED

ILLUSTRATION 4

FINANCIAL PLAN WORKSHEET

FEBRUARY

CHECK NUMBER	ITEM	1st FED.	STATE BK	RENT	ELECTRIC	TELEPHONE	GIFTS	HOUSEHOLD	CAR	STEREO	CHARGE	BILL	ENTERTAIN.	MISC.	SURPLUS
101	RENT			170 00											
102	1st FEDERAL	248 00													
103	MARY							145 00							
104	2ND FINANCE								60 00						
105	STATE BANK		75 00												
106	BILL											40 00			
107	UNITED FUND						10 00								
108	READERS DIG.													17 40	
109	SEARS										40 00				
110	ELECTRIC CO				26 50										
111	TELEPHONE					28 00									
112	VISA										64 00				
113	CITGO										74 00				
114	2ND FINANCE									21 00					
115	NITE CLUB												26 75		
116	REXALL													38 75	
117	CHURCH FUND						6 00								
118	SPORT SHOP													15 00	
119	CASH														29 60
		248 00	75 00	170 00	26 50	28 00	16 00	145 00	60 00	21 00	178 00	40 00	26 75	71 15	29 60

ILLUSTRATION 5

in each category.

The *actual* totals are then entered on the Financial Plan. On the following page, Illustration 6, this is already done.

With the actual amounts for SAVINGS and OBLIGATIONS entered, all that remains is to add the monthly column. That will give the ACTUAL TOTAL OBLIGATIONS. As you see, the Stevenson's total came to $1125.40.

Next, Bill and Mary entered their income which totalled $1155.00.

The final breath-taking step is to subtract the TOTAL OBLIGATIONS from the TOTAL INCOME to determine the amount of SURPLUS. The Stevenson's had a surplus of $29.60, which makes February a smashing success!

It is always interesting to note that, even with a surplus, some obligations will be greater than projected. Your first concern is to maintain a SURPLUS. Secondly, keep each OBLIGATION as near to your original projection as possible. When completing each month, take a moment to compare your projections with the actual dollars spent in each category.

A supply of 37 worksheets have been included in your WORKBOOK.

As we discussed earlier, Bill and Mary maintain a $25.00 buffer in their checking account. At the

FINANCIAL PLAN

SAVINGS

REAL & PROJECTED

YEAR	JAN	FEB	MAR	APR	MAY	JUN	JUL	AUG	SEPT	OCT	NOV	DEC
1ST FEDERAL SAVINGS & LOAN		248- 248⁰⁰	248-	248-	248-	248-						
STATE BANK		75- 75⁰⁰	75-	75-	75-	75-						

OBLIGATIONS

	JAN	FEB	MAR	APR	MAY	JUN	JUL	AUG	SEPT	OCT	NOV	DEC
RENT		170- 170⁰⁰	170-	170-	170-	170-						
ELECTRIC COMPANY		31- 26.50	31-	31-	31-	31-						
TELEPHONE		33- 28⁰⁰	33-	33-	33-	33-						
GIFTS AND CONTRIBUTIONS		16- 16⁰⁰	16-	16-	16-	16-						
HOUSEHOLD		165- 165⁰⁰	165-	165-	165-	165-						
CAR PAYMENT		60- 60⁰⁰	60-	60-	60-	60-				52-		
STEREO PAYMENT		21- 21⁰⁰	21-	21-	21-	21-			17-			
CHARGE PAYMENT VISA SEARS CITGO		180- 178⁰⁰	180-	180-	180-	180-						
SCHOOL EXPENSE - BILL		40- 40⁰⁰	40-	40-	40-	40-						
RECREATION AND ENTERTAINMENT		35- 26.75	35-	35-	35-	35-						
MISC		65- 71.15	65-	65-	65-	65-						
TOTAL OBLIGATIONS		1139- 1125.40	1139-	1139-	1139-	1139-						

NET INCOME

	JAN	FEB	MAR	APR	MAY	JUN	JUL	AUG	SEPT	OCT	NOV	DEC
BILL		1040- 1050⁰⁰	1040-	1040-	1040-	1040-			1060-			
MARY		115- 115⁰⁰	115-	115-	115-	115-				140-	140-	140-
TOTAL INCOME		1155- 1155⁰⁰	1155-	1155-	1155-	1155-						

SURPLUS

	JAN	FEB	MAR	APR	MAY	JUN	JUL	AUG	SEPT	OCT	NOV	DEC
		16- 29.60	16-	16-	16-	16-						

ILLUSTRATION NUMBER 6

end of February they wrote check number 119 to cash (surplus) for $29.60 which left a $25.00 balance (buffer) for March 1st (Illustration 4).

How much time was required? Certainly less than one hour on February 28th. Spending the $29.60 SURPLUS will take the Stevenson's more time than it took to complete their WORKSHEET.

Save your worksheets. Not only are they a must at tax time, but are very beneficial for future planning. Additional Financial Plan Worksheets can be reordered with the form in the back of this book.

Now you have the plan! It's a good one and Chapter Four will give you some great ideas on fine tuning. See you there!

REMEMBER . . .

GOOD MANAGEMENT IS EXTRA WORK, BUT IT'S ALSO WORK TO EARN NEEDLESSLY SPENT DOLLARS.

IDEAS AND NOTES
Sixty minutes of keeping up.

Chapter Four
Misfire: What if there isn't enough to go around?

If your Plan balances or only occasionally dips into the red, this chapter will help fine tune an already workable program. If, however, your Financial Plan sinks deeper into deficit each month, read this chapter carefully.

Let's begin by looking at the five financial danger signs. These signs will tell you when tough sledding lies ahead. Answer NO to these questions and you're probably in good shape. Using the information compiled in constructing your Financial Plan will be most helpful.

1. Do your outstanding *monthly* installment payments (credit cards and charge accounts) exceed 20% of your net income? Do not include your home mortgage.

2. Do you find it necessary to regularly use money from savings to pay monthly expenses?

3. Have you begun delaying payments that you once paid promptly?

4. Do you charge *everyday* expenses?

5. If necessary, would it take you more than one year to pay off all outstanding debts (not in-

including home mortgage)?

These are important warning signs. The decisions on where and what to cut are very personal. Only you can make that decision. No one else should. To make the wisest choices, let's talk about some of your options.

In Chapter One I mentioned that your goals will prove to be realistic when they are tested with your Financial Plan. Originally, Bill and Mary agreed that financial security ($2000.00 in the bank) would be one of their Short Term Goals. When their income was divided up there just wasn't enough money to go around. It would cost $167.00 each month for one year to meet this goal. It was their *mutual* decision to include this as a Medium Term Goal instead. The cost was now reduced over 60 months to $30.00 per month. A much more realistic goal. Bill and Mary did not eliminate their goal. They simply made it realistic for their particular situation.

Review your spending goals. Is there enough money to meet your Short Term Goal requirements *and* your monthly obligations, too? If not, which goals can be put off or delayed to ease your monthly cash flow?

Short Term Goals (wants and desires) will generally cause the greatest problems in balancing the new Financial Plan. That's because short term wants tend to exceed available income. That means that after monthly obligations are paid, *wants* seem to consume more than what is left. The ONLY way to deal with this type of situation is to curb your short term wants. Cut back on spending or spread them out over a longer time period so they become Medium or Long Term wants.

Are your Short and Medium Term Goals realistic?

Yes _____ No _____

By replacing a Short Term Goal as a Medium Term Goal your monthly cost is reduced 80%! However, do not put off 'til tomorrow what you can do today. *MORAL:* Savings is a must.

ANOTHER CONSIDERATION: Several years into our budget experience, Sandra and I developed a test phrase to help us determine if we could commit ourselves to a large purchase. "Maintain what you have before you expand." Translated, it means when there isn't enough money to go around, fix the old first. Each of us has a little mental list of things we know should be done. For example, the car has two bald tires.

That's a potentially dangerous situation, and each time you get into your car your mind says, "You really ought to get a couple of new tires." So what are you doing looking at that new motorcycle? Maintain what you have, the needed set of tires, before you expand with a new motorcycle.

Each time my neighbor mowed his lawn he would mentally note that his house needed storm windows. Every winter the cost of heating oil climbs higher and higher, but the acknowledged need for storm windows would only be triggered when he looked at his house while mowing, or when he wrote the heating oil check in the cold of winter.

A couple of years ago, Bill and Mary's beautiful wedding clock sat idle on its living room shelf. Obviously it needed to be cleaned and oiled, which in itself should be a small maintenance task. Since they had an electric kitchen clock they lived with the inconvenience of not knowing the time while they watched television. Their wedding gift only gathered dust.

Each time Bill brought up the idea of a new component stereo, Mary reminded him that she would prefer to have the clock properly repaired first. With that the conversation would end. Neither one getting any satisfaction out of their talk. It is interesting how easy it would be for Bill to have Mary's approval for the stereo. But, Bill never remembered to take the clock to the repair shop. Mary was certain it was Bill's responsibility, since he was the person that triggered her mind whenever he talked about a stereo.

From time to time, every person is reminded, if for only a moment, of something that should be attended to. Whether it's tires for the car, storm windows, or a clock to be repaired. The importance of these subtle reminders is that they get done in a consistent way. In other words, simply don't ignore them. To put it in another perspective, consider the new tires. If they are ignored and the motorcycle is purchased, the tires will most likely not get any better. Plans have been made so the motorcycle payments can be made without any apparent sacrifice. Then, to our consternation, the car is rendered unusable by tires that are flat and beyond repair. Wouldn't it be wiser to put off the motorcycle for three months or so until the tires are replaced and paid for?

In the case of my neighbor, he was upset by the high heating bills which he knew could be reduced with storm windows. He was equally upset by the fact that he had the money for the windows, but had spent it on a snowmobile which was rendered inoperative with a broken track. This becomes doubly unfortunate because the money to repair the snowmobile must be used for the additional fuel oil costs.

Maintain what you have (my neighbor's windows), before you expand (the snowmobile should be repaired and enjoyed).

You have already realized the Stevenson's had their wedding clock repaired since they have a stereo payment entered on their Financial Plan. What you may not know is how these three examples were resolved.

I advocate list making. First, because they organize priorities. By list making, you can visually commit yourself to acknowledge what is important. Keeping ideas in your head just doesn't cut it. It's easy to forget or recall ideas in an inappropriate order. Secondly, by writing down an idea you are freed to concentrate on other important things like problem solving or a project at hand, or simply relaxing.

Did you know a grocery list will save 10% on food bills by reducing impulse buying?

So far you have made three goal lists and from these you have constructed two savings lists. Using these will enable you to organize and direct your financial efforts in a predetermined direction. A direction you have planned.

But, what about those little things? All those loose ends?

To accommodate a solution, I introduce you to the TO IT LIST. A TO IT LIST is for the things you want to make time to get around to. Not goals, but projects you want or need to complete. It's a grab bag of activities, a way to gather those personal loose ends together. A catchall, if you will. A potpourri of loose ends.

A TO IT LIST is different for each person and each situation. The one similarity, however, is that a TO IT LIST will free up creative energy and allow the user more free time. It makes any Financial Plan (and home) function with less effort and stress.

A TO IT LIST is not completed by sitting down over a cup of coffee and jotting down everything in twenty minutes. That's a Short Term Goals list.

A TO IT LIST is done over a longer time period. If you're getting into your car and the bald tires pop into your mind for the tenth time, go straight to your TO IT LIST and write it down.

When you're mowing your lawn and realize storm windows would save heat and money, let the mower run, but write it down on your TO IT LIST.

My neighbor should have stopped his mower, walked straight to his desk and put *storm windows* on his TO IT LIST. Then, finished mowing.

The Stevenson's agreed to do the clock repair

before the stereo purchase.

How are your tires?

Refer to your TO IT LIST when you review your Financial Plan. Most people using a TO IT LIST will use their surplus when money is needed to complete the project.

As you build your TO IT LIST, do one item each day (or week). No more, no less. On the first of each week take item one (not 2 or 4) and do what's necessary to complete it by week's end. If any project requires more than a few dollars to complete, consider placing it on one of your goal lists. If it's storm windows, it may be necessary to nail plastic over the windows this year and put the storms on next summer.

The whole idea is, *maintain* what you have before you expand.

What does this have to do with balancing your Financial Plan? Maintaining what you have will, in most cases, cost less than expanding. Give it some thought. Also, when you expand, you now have two things to maintain. What you had and what you have acquired by expanding.

Below are more ideas that will help keep your Financial Plan working and out of the red.

1. As a *couple,* agree on your goals. This is normally done when goal lists are completed.

If there is any disagreement, try to compromise.

2. Don't start cutting away at one category just because it looks too big. A major expense can not be cut simply because it appears so big when the amount is computed. FOOD or HOUSEHOLD is a category that most families will try to slash first. If that item is cut too low, the result could become an impossibility and the money manager won't be able to manage. If the family refuses to eat beans in place of steaks, the cook can't be expected to feed the family on a "beans" budget.

3. Each year, a family's life brings its own special highs and disasters. If your Plan is unyielding it will break from its own inflexibility. Try to have a flexible Plan and include everyone involved in its success.

4. Try to provide everyone involved with an amount they can spend as they see fit. It may have to be small, but if the entire family cooperates the amounts can become larger. Also, this helps prevent nagging and bickering over money. There won't be any need to dip into the grocery money for lunch with friends or to conceal the real amount of the paycheck in order to have a little money for an evening out with the guys. Instead, every-

thing will be open and above board.

5. When reductions in spending are unavoidable, consider each category of expense.
Some examples might be:

RENT: Can you get by with less space? If you
are single, can you share with someone to cut
costs?

HEAT: Consider insulation, storm windows,
or cleaning the furnace.

REPAIR SERVICE: These have increased
400% from past years. Can you do more
repairs for yourself? Talk to friends and find
out how they have reduced costs. Visit your
library and public utilities. They have many
money saving ideas for reducing costs.

6. Don't make a big deal over little things. Instead, look for trends and discuss these
with everyone involved.

7. Be willing to re-evaluate priorities. You may
see a lot of money going for entertainment
and clothing while the family complains that a
new couch is needed or the TV is shot. A
family conference may be in order to estab-
lish what is essential and what is a luxury.
Keep everyone involved and remain flexible.

8. If you become crunched, visit your creditors.
Explain to them what you are doing to work
out your debts. Seek to re-adjust your pay-

ment schedule if necessary. Show them your Financial Plan. Protect your credit!

9. If you have several installment loans, consider a consolidation loan, but only from a credit union, savings and loan, or bank (not a high cost loan company). This will consolidate your outstanding debts and enable you to make only one monthly payment at a greatly reduced amount.

   NOTE: When using a consolidation loan, it is known that four out of five people will replace their monthly debt load within 24 months. It should then be obvious that for a consolidation loan to be effective, taking on additional install- ment payments must not be done until the con- solidation loan is reduced. With this statistic in mind, it is important to remember that you simply can't borrow your way into solvency. A consol- idation loan is an excellent tool, but like most things, it must be used with a sound plan in mind.

10. The best Financial Plan may run aground be- cause of family emotional situations. A spouse may be extremely thrifty to the point of penny pinching. Perhaps psychological difficulties result in gambling, over generosity, or heedless spending even after agreeing to a plan to pay off debts. The person involved may be unable to understand the problem

and may need professional help to eliminate the cause. When this is necessary, it can be found through a Family Social Service Agency listed in the telephone book. However, most people, once they recognize the possibilities of a sound Financial Plan, *can* eliminate their money problems.

11. An important part of your Financial Plan must be a special place where your records, bills, and worksheets are to be kept. A desk is best (but not required) for organizing bill paying and maintaining your up-to-date Financial Plan. It is most important that you try to provide such a place.

    A cardboard box just isn't the way to organize bills and worksheets. If space in the family room is a problem, consider a corner of the living room, bedroom, kitchen, or hall. What about a desk in the basement? Financial planning is important and it requires that each family make room for it.

12. Do remember, it's more worthwhile to save one dollar than to add one dollar to your present income. To add a dollar requires your income to increase a *minimum* of $1.15 before taxes. When spending is reduced one dollar you recover a full dollar. Even when you bring in more income you're

caught by higher taxes. Your best recourse is better management of the cash you have.

13. Most people who find themselves in financial hot water are simply overextended. That means they have used money that should have gone into savings, or have taken money out of savings, or worse yet, they have borrowed to cover *everyday* expenses. If you find yourself overextended, *reduce spending.* Stop using credit and try not to take on new installment payments. There is life without credit cards! Let your spending cool until you have a SURPLUS.

   An older gentleman once summed it up this way, "Trouble is, everybody wants instant everything."

14. After using your Financial Plan for several months, you will know the value of looking for trends. Look at each expense and determine if it's on target or if you might need to adjust your projection. If it's a trouble maker, it will do so with a trend first.

15. In trouble shooting your new Plan, it isn't important to attempt a precise record at the start. Unless you have always kept exact records, you will have had to estimate to determine your projections. Relax, later it will be possible to be more precise.

16. Should you begin to feel the heat of over-extension, re-examine your priorities. You may not be able to save for a vacation and a microwave at the same time.

17. To keep savings on schedule, consider using devices such as automatic payroll deductions or monthly transfers from checking to savings.

Do you see yourself side-tracked by any of these 17 financial road blocks? Any one will undermine an effective Financial Plan and certainly prevent yours from being all that it can be. Everyday people loose more and more of what they've worked for... just by not seeing the erosion caused by seemingly unimportant attitudes and habits. Never underestimate the obvious... having a special place for your financial records is equally important to a consistent savings program. Also, to expect financial success without first setting worthwhile goals just can't and will not happen.

Many people have a mistaken idea. They have the notion that life is played much like any game. In baseball, players practice to improve their skills in preparation for next weeks game. A good player practices his throwing, his catching, his running, and his batting. If this weeks game proves not to be a victory, well, it was a good try and next weeks contest will surely be better. Practice makes perfect, or so it goes! The financial game is different. There is no practice session. It's now and it's for keeps! There is no next week. A bad investment, an unforeseen emergency, or an untimely purchase not fully thought through can put you years behind your ability to ever catch up. Sometimes you will never be able to recover. IT IS important to plan ahead (by setting worthwhile goals) and IT IS important to weigh each financial move against your Financial Plan before you act. In a financial sense, you don't have any practice tries... without paying a price.

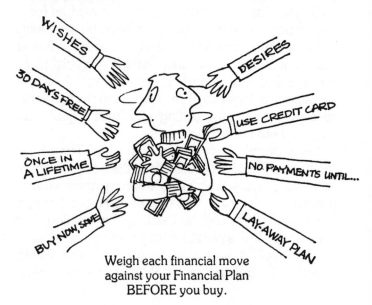

Weigh each financial move
against your Financial Plan
BEFORE you buy.

This chapter deals with the mystery of not having enough money to go around. It's rather like standing there on payday, trying to stuff your hard earned money into your pockets while all these people are trying to keep you from doing it! They want to get as much of your cash as they can. That's what our economy is all about... and that can be a problem.

I call this the problem of realization. The reasons are many, and the conversation can go any of two ways. The first goes like this, "I make good money, I pay my bills on time and I feel I'm doing a pretty good job in that department; but, sometimes I wonder if I can do better. Am I doing all I am capable of?". This is an excellent reason to begin financial planning. It will enable you to "fine-tune" your spending, or better, enable you to take stock of your total financial situation.

The second conversation goes something like this, "I'm talk'n hot water! Real discomfort between me and payday!". The difference is obvious. The first situation has control, but wants to maximize the return. The second situation is a real dilemma. This person will need to re-evaluate his or her entire program to develop the discipline necessary to follow a sound Financial Plan. Whatever your situation, the realization becomes obvious. Whether it's necessary to slap the hands that try to pick your pockets on payday or say no to the enticing ads placed in front of you hundreds of times every day. The answer isn't a budget that tells how you have already spent your money, but rather a Financial Plan that enables you to determine how you plan to spend your money.

If you buy this idea, you'll be able to get your pocket full of money home to better *decide* who get's what part of your money pie. In this chapter, that becomes another problem.

Before you're able to say how you plan to spend (or not spend) your money, you must know what is important to you. Sounds simple! There is an old saying that goes, "If you don't know where it is you want to go, you'll likely end up someplace else." Most people just don't know. To make it in this economy, it's absolutely essential to set personal spending goals. This continues to be the single most important step toward financial success anyone can take... yet so few people ever take the time to figure it out.

In our society we take note of the disadvantaged and applaud any group or agency that lends a helping hand. For each of us, having an income means being able to take care of our needs... proper food, secure shelter, and adequate clothing. As you review your goals in the context of this chapter, listen for the truth in this cliche, "Wants expand to consume the available resources!". It will be worthwhile to ask yourself this simple question. Which goals are wants and which are needs?

Needs are the unavoidable costs of just being on this planet. Not only do they include housing, food, and clothing, but in our modern society they also include taxes, medical care, transportation, and utilities of some sort. Fortunately the needs list is short, but none-the-less costly. I don't know anyone doing handsprings over paying these unavoidable and necessary obligations. Wants, on the other hand are endless! A quick look at my goals list proves that. The trick is being able to recognize wants from needs so as not to jeopardize your financial future. For some, life may seem like a game, but not where your money is concerned. As you review your obligations (and not-so-monthly ones) ferret out the wants until after your needs are taken care of.

Ferreting out costly wants would seem as easy as attaining your first goal. Well, not really. Anyone who hasn't found a surplus at the end of their Financial Plan by now has only one place left to look. Actually I have discussed several options beyond the 17 numbered in this chapter. Of all POSSIBLE solutions to the dilemma of finding that elusive surplus, there remains only one choice. That is, more money or fewer wants. Since wants expand to consume the available resources, more money will prove to be only a temporary solution... at best. Wants vs. needs is all that remains. Why is that such a big deal? Well, needs provide for our existence while wants provide our LIFE STYLE. That is the bottom line. It's much like the man who is told by his doctor that either he stops smoking or he won't need next years calendar. Consider the person who begins an aggressive health program AFTER the heart attack. It wasn't until his life style was threatened that real action took place.

Few people will take action simply because it seems like a good idea... even though it benefits their own best interests. Why? Because, until there is a direct threat to their life style there isn't a strong enough motivation to do so. We all have heard the stories of the smoker who couldn't quit but suddenly stopped cold turkey... or the obese person leading a sedentary *life style* who, over night, got the message and started exercising with the determination of a marathon runner!

It's not until we come face to face with a possible change in our financial or social life style that serious consideration is given to our financial wants... and any change in our financial life style will undeniably have a corresponding effect on our social life style. To put ourselves back on safe financial footing, it may be necessary to identify that which is a *want* and that which is our most pressing *need*. Wants vs. needs are real heavy weights in our society in-as-much as they are reinforced by their old ally, social pressure (peer pressure to our kids). If the answer to that illusive Surplus has brought you to this point, you now have the only answer left... the best of luck in making these difficult choices.

NEEDS vs. WANTS

The way to financial peace of mind goes beyond examples and illustrations. It's not in how much you earn, but in what you do with what you earn. *Wanting* more and more income won't get what you want, but managing what you have will. It's not living by some mystical dream, but rather planning how you are going to live.

Your Financial Plan will tell you your financial story. Whether or not you like the story, you will have to listen to it. Whether or not this version of your financial condition is what you want, it is the true version. Be determined, be honest and you will learn the *art* of making your paycheck last.

REMEMBER ..
To do it you gotta get around TO IT.

IDEAS AND NOTES
What if there isn't enough to go around?

Chapter Five
I can see clearly now, but . . .

As you continue using your Financial Plan and become familiar with it's operation, questions will arise. Questions about evaluating your new information, your Plan, and making it work harder for you. In this chapter we'll discuss the most frequently asked questions.

In dealing with your special questions, the first action should be to re-read the section that deals with your problem area. Next, consider your situation. As long as your resulting solution is reasonable, try it. There just aren't any hard and fast rules.

1. QUESTION: *When evaluating the success of my Plan, what are the indicators that show I'm doing the right things?*

ANSWER: There is no firm yardstick to measure your progress, but there are two basic indicators. Both are related to trends that develop month by month. The first, SURPLUS, is the most important. If you consistently have a surplus, your Plan is doing what it should be expected to do. Even when your surplus is small, it's still successful.

Chapter four is devoted to ways of insuring a surplus. Review this chapter if you don't have a positive surplus any two consecutive months.

Also, by not writing that check for your monthly surplus you can cause your Plan to go into the *red* the following month. The importance of this was discussed in the last few pages of Chapter Two. Review this section from time to time.

What about the months where there is a surplus but several Obligations exceed their original projections? That's when our second indicator, fine tuning, is necessary. If actual costs continually exceed projections by more than 15%, a conference with everyone involved is in order. Talk it over, openly discuss ways of cutting back to return to your projections. If the original projections are based on estimates, it may be necessary to re-evaluate these figures.

By discussing these projections, everyone involved is alerted to the overages. An *honest* and *tactful* discussion will provide ideas and a new resolve to keep each projection on target.

Fine tuning, zeroing in on each obligation is important. But, the bottom line - *Surplus* - should be of first concern. If the surplus is, by your estimate, unusually large, it might be a good idea to increase savings. Too large a surplus leads to complacency which in itself makes your Financial Plan less than it can be. A reasonable surplus is necessary. The amount that is acceptable is up to you.

If your TO IT LIST is long, you may want to have a slightly larger surplus.

Generally, a surplus of 3-5% of your net income is a good average (3% of a net income of $1000 is $30.00). If surplus is more than 5%, think about it. A little extra in savings will go a long way on rainy days. When it's continually less than 3%, zero in on fine tuning each obligation.

2. QUESTION: *When evaluating the success of my Plan, what is the most important aspect to consider?*

ANSWER: GOALS! Without a goal no Plan will be effective. No matter how elaborate it might be, no matter how well intentioned, it will not be effective or lasting without first having a goal. Goals provide direction, priorities, and momentum. Without these, there is no lasting reason to stay with a program. Without first having the goal there can be no planned success. *Absolutely!* Your Financial Plan is the *means* by which you achieve the goals you set for yourself.

In evaluating your progress on a monthly basis you can see where *Surplus* and fine tuning are important. What about the long run? Next year and the following? The top priority of every Financial Plan must be a consistent savings goal. It may only be $5.00 each month, but the consistency is what it's all about. I don't think it's necessary to go into a discussion of the needs and virtues of saving for tomorrow, but it is well to consider the eventualities that life can deal each of us. Realize that a savings program can spell the difference in how we survive a momentary crisis or temporary setback.

In short, when evaluating your Plan, be confident your goals are worthy. They reflect how you want to direct your time and resources. Then, be certain your priorities include absolute consistency in your two savings programs.

3. QUESTION: *I just started my Financial Plan and already have $100.00 in my Short Term Savings. Yesterday my auto insurance bill arrived for $300.00. What do I do now that I am $200.00 short?*

ANSWER: What did you do before you had a savings account (which now has $100.00 in it)? Did you cut back on a number of monthly obligations to free up the needed cash? Since you are just getting your Plan started, you may want to do just that.

Some people use a different approach. If they

are saving $150.00 a month in their Short Term Savings Account, they will save $1800 each year. In order to get their fledgling plan off the ground, one option is to borrow $1800 from the bank and repay it at $150.00 per month. The interest paid on this loan will be partially offset by the interest earned on the savings.

A better way might be to borrow only $500.00 or $600.00 on a 1-year-note to give you *seed money* for your account, instead of borrowing the full $1800 in this example.

Another possible solution is a "Peter to Paul" loan. Borrow the $200.00 you're short from your Long Term Savings Account. You are robbing Peter to pay Paul, and Peter *is* your opportunity account. I favor one of the other methods since this arrangement can be habit forming. However, a "Peter to Paul" loan is an option. These are three possible solutions. Consider your situation, then look at your options.

4. QUESTION: *Our Financial Plan had a surplus eight months out of twelve. What suggestions do you have regarding the four months there was no surplus?*

ANSWER: Upon reviewing your Plan, I noticed that if you had paid nothing more than the amount *projected* for charge payments and medical, you would have had a perfect 12 months. If you are free of medical bills for several months and get a $50.00 office call, pay only the $20.00 you projected. Next month, pay $20.00 and on the third month the final $10.00.

Charge accounts do require more attention because of minimum payment requirements. Still, that's a good reason to limit time payments. Because of the advantages that go with charge accounts, it's a good idea to treat them with a special watchfulness.

While reviewing the Financial Plan used in this question, it will be helpful to mention one other observation. The Short Term Savings Account includes a monthly amount toward insurance. Since a particular insurance payment was only $75.00 it was paid from the primary checking account and shown as a *Misc.* obligation on the Financial Plan. That's fine because the insurance payment was made and all is well. However, notice how *Misc.* jumped from $45.00 to $120.00 while your savings dropped terribly ($75.00) for the month. When making *future projections*, entries like this can get a little confusing - if not downright scarry.

Therefore, when making payments that normally should come from savings, enter the payment in savings on your Worksheet - not in *Miscellaneous*, even if you pay it by check from your primary account.

5. QUESTION: *Each month I total my FInancial Plan and determine my Surplus. Then, I write a check for that sum. Since I have the amount of Surplus recorded on my Financial Plan and check register, Why do I have a Surplus column on my worksheet?*

ANSWER: First, your *Surplus* should equal your checkbook balance (plus any *Buffer*). Once your check for *Surplus* has been written, your checking balance will be zero (or the amount of your *Buffer* if you use one). If there is a difference between your checkbook balance and *Surplus* amount, use your checkbook balance since it is reduced to zero each month (assuming your math is correct).

Why do you have a *Surplus* column on your Worksheet? Because your worksheet is actually a large check register, with a couple of modifications. Instead of simply subtracting checks and adding deposits (as you do with a check register), your worksheet also categorizes checks. However, like your check register, continuity is maintained by check number.

Another advantage offered by the Worksheet is at tax time. Necessary checks are easy to find if first you refer to the category (for instance Medical or Mortgage), then locate checks by number.

More about this later.

6. QUESTION: *You have talked a lot about list making and its value in selecting the best option when making a financial decision. Would you briefly outline this process?*

ANSWER: Volumes have been written on the decision making process. When all is said and done, a five step method remains. Whether we are aware of it or not, each decision we make is in some way achieved through this five step process. To illustrate, imagine you have a large heating oil bill that must be paid within 30 days. The decision making process says:

1. DEFINE YOUR PROBLEM
   The best problem solving is done on paper. By writing you're able to view the problem in a form other than passing thoughts. "I have a huge $600.00 oil bill to pay in 30 days with only $200.00 available."

2. CONSIDER YOUR CAPABILITIES AND STRONG POINTS
   a. Available cash: Checking, Savings, Cash
   b. What bills can be put off or minimum paid?
   c. Money coming in the next 30 days?
   d. Assess your strong points: Overtime, part-time work, etc. Now may be the time to sell your neighbor your antique car he

has wanted.

    e.   Ask the Oil Co. about time payments because you can budget $110.00 per month for fuel oil.

3. IDENTIFY THE PROBLEMS IN REACHING YOUR GOAL
   a. You have the flu.

4. CONSIDER YOUR OPTIONS
   a. Take $200.00 out of savings and/or . . .
   b. Use the $50.00 cash on hand and/or . . .
   c. Minimum payments on current bills . . . (an additional $75.00)
   d. The Oil Co. will go along with payment over 90 days.

5. SELECT BEST OPTION
   a. Pay over 90 days. Use the $200.00 in savings for payment #1.

From the information given, how would you make the next two installments?

1. DEFINE the problem
2. CONSIDER your capabilities and strong points
3. IDENTIFY problems in reaching your goal
4. CONSIDER your options
5. SELECT best option

7. QUESTION: *Would you review the ways to determine if your goals are realistic and what can be done if you discover they aren't?*

ANSWER: Assume your only goal is to pay your monthly bills. First you will total your bills to see if there is enough cash to go around. If there is, you have a realistic goal. If not, consider your options: consolidation loan, monthly installments, etc. (Chapter Four stuff). But, let's imagine your goal lists are ten each and you could add a bunch more. Well, the conclusion is obvious. By making the three goal lists, *you can* plainly identify what you're after. If it's heavily money oriented and you don't have that kind of cash, realizing it now will enable you to begin planning for it. Maybe you can't achieve everything as soon as you thought, but now you can arrange your priorities and do something positive to bring you closer to those goals . . . even if *closer* is now five years away.

One final point: If you really want a vacation home (for example) and find that once you have placed a dollar value on it, you realize the impossibility of saving for your retreat. Don't shrug it off as the impossible dream. It might be that actual saving can't begin for 8 or 9 years. Perhaps the vacation home will result from the equity in your present home. Shelving a goal until the children are out of school can be smart planning.

8. QUESTION: *What is the biggest mistake today's wage earners make in managing their money?*
ANSWER: Not planning. Taking a passive approach to money management. Too many people (like their parents before them) assume hard work will automatically pay off with a better job, more income, the house, and everything that goes with The Great American Dream. The times have changed and the rules are different. Young and old alike just aren't geared to using a cash monitoring plan (a Financial Plan if your prefer) to get a clear picture of current income and outflow.

Another error begins to appear as people react to these new rules. Simply put, you just don't spend money for the sake of saving on taxes. It doesn't work and you could go broke doing it. There has got to be a better reason than saving on taxes to spend money. Tax saving should only be a side benefit.

9. QUESTION: *How will this program help me at tax time?*
ANSWER: Your Financial Plan will be a great help at tax time. Not only do you have a record by

check number of where your money has gone, but it is already divided by category on your Worksheet. Talk to your tax preparer to determine which category will be of benefit to you. Depending on your situation, a portion of your rent, mortgage interest, utilities, medical bills, charitable contributions, charge account interest, auto expense, child care, and more may be tax deductible.

As your cancelled checks are returned from your bank, staple them to the receipt from which they where paid. Then, put these in a manila envelope. Many people label their envelopes, one for each column of their Worksheet.

Give your tax preparer the following:
1) W-2 Form from your employer
2) The IRS tax guide (arrives in the mail)
3) Your Financial Plan stapled to the Worksheets.
4) Envelopes containing your cancelled checks and receipts.
5) Bank savings account interest earned statement.
6) Don't forget your Short Term Savings Account. Include your copy of your *paid* property tax bill, insurance bills, organization dues, bank interest,

tuition, heating oil bills, etc. Put these in separate envelopes marked Savings.
These are the big obligations you save a little each month for.

That's it! As you can see, you can easily maximize your deductions with good record keeping. With these good records you will also minimize the time spent collecting the information.

10. QUESTION: *What if I don't have a regular income? I work on commission and my income varies month to month.*

ANSWER: In situations where income varies, your Financial Plan will really be a benefit. Deposit your commission in a savings or interest bearing checking account. Each month withdraw the amount you have projected as your total obligations.

Using this method has a couple of nice advantages. First, you will be receiving interest on the maximum amount of money right up to the time you need it for your monthly obligations. Secondly, with a sound Financial Plan, it will be easy to know what your dollar needs are for the months down the road.

One note of caution. With an irregular income it is very important to take care when estimating your future obligations so that during the low income months the cash is there.

11. QUESTION: *What do you think of the use of credit cards?*

ANSWER: Credit is a valuable asset, but becomes a liability with overuse.

Credit is important to have in this day and age. It offers a reserve that you can fall back on when an emergency arises. It offers the flexibility that enables you to take advantage of sales and avoid future price increases. Durable goods like refrigerators, washing machines, and cars can be financed as necessary. Vacations, presents, everyday expenses, and purchases under $25.00 shouldn't be paid with credit (assuming they are not for business reasons).

It must always be remembered that *most* financial crises start with the unwise use of credit. Here are some safety rules for taking full advantage of credit while keeping out of hot water.

1. Don't seek more credit than you need. A critical analysis of your Financial Plan will give you a pretty good feel for your credit requirements.

Even though you think you will use it only in an emergency, the temptation is always there. Also, unused credit is sometimes counted against you when you seek large credit, i.e., home or auto loan, since use of this unused credit could possibly affect your ability to repay the loan you now seek.

2. Don't expand your use of credit simply because your income increases. It is far better to use extra income to reduce your present debt load.

3. Keep the number of non-business credit cards to a minimum. Credit counselors advise their clients to *carry* no more than two cards. The more you have, the more the psychological tendency to overspend. The other advantage is not so obvious. Credit cards in most states use interest of about 18% on the first $500.00, then 12%. The fewer cards you use, the less interest you will pay on the same amount of dollars charged.

4. *Never* charge any item under $25.00. A significant amount of bad debt stems from small purchases . . . that probably would never have been made if the person had paid cash.

5. *Never* charge everyday expenses. *NEVER!*

6. Use your Financial Plan to determine the amount you can comfortably afford to devote to credit card repayment. Then monitor your credit

purchases carefully so your comfort level is never exceeded.

7. Excluding mortgage payments, loan repayment (credit card and charge account) should not exceed 20% of an individual's or couple's take-home pay.

Use credit wisely and it will offer you a great deal of flexibility. You will realize that your income will indeed go farther and yield a greater return.

12. QUESTION: *As a new money manager, my financial situation is clearly improving. That's great. How else can I make my pay check go farther?*

ANSWER: The ways to make your paycheck go farther are abundant and limited only by your inclination. Here are a few common ways to help you get started.

The cash discount is a real money saver used by all successful people. It works two ways. First, when buying *anything* ask for a 10% discount. Sound ridiculous?

Hold on! I know people who expect 20%. I am only suggesting ten until you gain confidence.

The other angle of the cash discount goes like this. Suppose you plan to paint your house. You missed the traditional paint sale in September. Go to the paint store, pick out the color you want and explain what you are about to do (the painting, not the money savings). Now, look the owner or manager (never a clerk) in the eye and say, "If you will sell me paint at the contractors discount, I'll give you 100% of my business from now on!". You have just saved 20%-40%. That makes your paycheck go farther.

When buying large items such as appliances and furniture, shop around and always ask, "and what is my discount?". Be serious, and you won't go to three stores before you have what you're after at a big savings. I say three stores because two will certainly give you 10%. It's the third store that will save you 15% to 20%. This money saving idea is used by dollar-wise people, and it will work for you.

Locally owned, neighborhood stores are most receptive to discounting. Particularly if they are assured you will be a dependable, *repeat* customer.

I know a fellow who saves 10% at his local hardware store using this approach. Not only does he save 10%, but since he is a frequent, repeat buyer, the store *bills* him each month. That's convenient. He has assured me his average discount is much higher since he is offered super deals on damaged, discontinued, and returned merchandise.

However, don't think for a moment that major stores won't give discounts. They can't be as flexible and won't include all store items, but because of their buying power, their sales offer tremendous savings. In larger cities, chain stores have outlets where slightly damaged, discontinued, and overstock merchandise is sold at up to 50% off.

When we talked about list making, I said that a grocery list will save 10% by eliminating impulse buying. Additionally, shopping once or twice a month will reduce exposure to impulse buying. Unless you have a particular purchase in mind, try to stay out of stores. Window shopping can be expensive.

Another money saving, paycheck stretching idea is *Do It Yourself*. Not everything, but a few things. Hardware stores and lumber yards give free advice. Utility companies and magazines are full of ideas and directions. Neighbors are surprisingly ingenious. Talk to them and you'll have fun at the same time.

10% here, 20% there! It all adds up. More savings are there and one fact is certain. People make their paycheck go farther by simply *asking*. Try it!

As you can see financial planning is no mystery

or just for the old and rich. The entire economy has undergone fantastic changes in the past few years. Clearly, it will never be the same as it was. Having your Financial Plan will provide the means to weather the economic downturns and take advantage of the better times that are sure to follow.

Your Goal Lists and Financial Plan are very much like a road map without which you would certainly make many wrong turns and likely end up at the wrong destination. You now have them to help you get to your destination.

You have the tools you need to set your course, keep control, and make your paycheck last!

REMEMBER . . .

THERE ARE ALWAYS POSSIBILITIES.

IDEAS AND NOTES
I can see clearly now, but . . .

Mail Order Information

MAKE YOUR PAYCHECK LAST by Harold Moe, 2nd Edition, 103 pages, 15 illustrations. A complete, step by step guide that shows how to fine tune or trouble shoot any financial situation. The book includes a complete financial plan, setting goals that work, the five financial danger signs, proven techniques for transforming financial problems to financial success. Details rules for using credit cards successfully and dozens of dollar stretching ideas. Focuses on personal and family finance.................................**$4.95**

MAKE YOUR PAYCHECK LAST WORKBOOK, 39 pages, padded. Contains financial planning layout sheets in large 11 x 14 colored format and three years of personal worksheets. This is the companion workbook to *Make Your Paycheck Last* and is designed to carry you through the easy step by step program.......................**$5.95**

TO IT ORGANIZER, 52 pages, padded. A people-proven method of prioritizing that endless list of things that can . . . but never seem to get done. Formatted "weekly" with priority rating and check-off notation. Enables user to see where they have been and where they are going at a glance. The ideal, "I really have to get around to it" solution.
....................................**$3.49**

Make Your Paycheck Last Workbook and To It Organizer together **(save $2.49)**..........**$6.95**

Financial Stress. Business people, social security recipients, and commission wage earners all share a common problem. These people do not receive a timely and consistent paycheck. As a result, they must deal with a higher level of stress due to their fluctuating finances. Tests reveal these groups must deal with higher stress levels.

LEARN TO RELAX: A 14 DAY PROGRAM by John D. Curtis, Ph.D. and Richard A. Detert, 2nd Edition, 112 pages, 18 photographs, is a simple, easy-to-follow book that teaches realistic stress management and relaxation. The book includes relaxation exercises, motivational techniques, questions and answers, and a chapter on the new and exciting *instant relaxation* method...... **$4.95**

FINANCIAL STRATEGY KIT. The only complete financial strategy kit available today. Includes, *"Make Your Paycheck Last"*, the companion *"Workbook"*, and the *"To It Organizer"*. Everything in one powerful package. Ideal for gifts, graduations, weddings, and retirements. **(save $1.44)**........................ **$12.95**

FINANCIAL STRATEGY KIT with *LEARN TO RELAX* book **(save $3.39)**............ **$15.95**

Mail Order Form

Books		Quantity	Amount
Make Your Paycheck Last	**$4.95** _____		_____
Make Your Paycheck Last **Workbook**	**5.95** _____		_____
To It **Organizer**	**3.49** _____		_____
Workbook with **Organizer** (save 2.49)	**6.95** _____		_____
Learn To Relax: A 14 Day Program	**4.95** _____		_____

Financial Strategy Kit (save 1.44)   **12.95**_____ _____
> *Make Your Paycheck Last*
> *Make Your Paycheck Last* **Workbook**
> *To It* **Organizer**

Financial Strategy Kit (save 3.39)   **15.95**_____ _____
> *Make Your Paycheck Last*
> *Make Your Paycheck Last* **Workbook**
> *To It* **Organizer**
> *Learn To Relax: A 14 Day Program*

Total Price of Items _____

Shipping and Handling **$2.00**
(not applicable to *To It Organizer*)

5% Sales Tax for Wisconsin Residents _____

Total _____

SHIP TO: Name _____

(Please Print) Address _____

City _____ State _____ Zip _____

☐ Check or Money Order enclosed

☐ Please Charge my Mastercard account

☐ Please Charge my Visa account

Charge Account Number _____

My Card Expires _____

_____

Authorized Signature

Send your order to: HARSAND PRESS, P.O. BOX 515, Holmen, WI 54636